Caramel Love

Patricia Sadri

BookLeaf Publishing

Presentation by *BookLeaf Publishing*

Web: www.bookleafpub.com

E-mail: info@bookleafpub.com

ISBN: 9789357219778

First edition 2023

To my late mother, Luciana Sadri... Until we meet again.

ACKNOWLEDGEMENT

A big Thank You to My father - Phiroz Sadri & My elder sister - Natasha Michelle for supporting me always. To my beautiful nieces, Lucia and Olessia, my angels.

To all my friends for showing me that life is more than just work. You all mean the world to me.

PREFACE

Caramel Love is the sweet combination of caramel mixed with love. So sweet that life becomes the eternal love of a true mother.

Every poem that you read will create in you the imagery of love. The power of silence and the depths of wisdom that already flows within your heart. You will feel the undercurrents of deeper emotions flowing within the lines. Even though these poems are dedicated to my mother, its words will relate to you. My heart goes out to each one of you who finds my book worthy of your time.

May you let in the abundance of warmth and heaven's blessings. Here's wishing you a loving day as you turn every page to a new life.

Where you Lived

Hearts can break like a sinking ship
Like the ocean welling up in my throat
With undercurrents flowing deep within
Sending out ripples of a journey left halfway

You may have gone, never to return
But what's left behind are the footprints of your love
The place where you sat, the table where you dined
Your love remains in the memories of where you lived

Peeking through My Unseen Clouds

Where you lived marked my heart
And it glowed in the dark
You were light from treasure chests
Like the rays that made their way
Through gemstones, gold and pearls

But when you left, all treasure chests were shut
And in the end, darkness remained
The void that I held onto
Empty cyclones from the years of old

Where you lived, in my heart
That journey had an end
Like the burning sun that had to set
Like the dimming twilight with the rising moon

Like unseen clouds of remorse
You were gone high up there
Far away from my reach
And you saw me, from up above
Peeking through my unseen clouds

Let It All Go

And yet, peeking through my unseen clouds
Invisible strength and perseverance
Was a power blessed by you
To the silence left behind

This power wrapped the wind beneath
Along with it the earth, the sand, the leaves
And pink and white petals swirled around
They were lighter than the air

But resistance sat upon my throne
A flowing river of vengeful ripples
Hid brewing within my soul
Hitting against unwavering rocks
The stubbornness of not letting go
Strangely, your power sought a way in
Like water that knew its course

The petals, the leaves, the wind, and earth
Engulfed my soul within its reach
Swirling around me, high and low
The sounds of mother nature whispered
Leave it all behind, let it all go

A Dim-Lit Past

And while I had to let it all go
Who I was, I thought I was
My core was primed with the past
The pain, the tears, the fears

But the wind, high and low, took its course
And gently said to me

"When peaceful streams of peace
flow beneath your wings
Why fan the flames of uncertainty?

When the sun's unquenchable thirst
drinks and eats the rays your doubts
and heatwaves of your vengeful spirit
Why oil your night lamp with a dim-lit past?"

On the Verge of Crumbling

5

But with this dim-lit past
Did I learn to grow up
How could my core just let it all go?

To which the winds continued to swirl
And in its gentle breeze said to me

"When high waves bow at your feet
Commanding where the wind should blow
Why seek shallow tides that recede?
There's no need to knock on open doors
Break through your walls
They're on the verge of crumbling."

Rivers of Stillness

I was on the verge of crumbling
All these years with half a broken back
Burdened by a stumbling stupor
But my fort I kept upright
The only bricks that kept me from breaking

Why must I break through these walls?
They're pillared upon my rage
A power strong enough to get me through
They're the lessons taught by the past
A childhood for which I never asked

To which the winds gently said

"How do you know of imminent death?
The soul, the body - connected but unmet
They separate like the cycles of the moon
Sometimes vanishing, and then reappearing"

"And yours is the sun and the wind
For the roaring thunders from childhood storms
Are meant to calm down with rivers of stillness"

Crushed or Ripped

Rivers of stillness? I thought to myself
Where have they been, no rumours, no word
I tried and tested my feelings, my void
And rarely I've dug the deep wounds inside

So fearful was I, the past would catch up
The soundbox of violence would play on repeat
That deep down I locked each floor
No key could they find nor knobs to a door

The wind told me then, I'd ran out of luck
"There's running no more nor finding refuge
For feelings but are, keys to each door
Your story ends not falling to the floor

The places I hid, the windows I closed
They're all in the wind, the pages that flipped
The ones that you wrote, crushed and ripped"

Shine Instead

Crushed and Ripped? I asked the wind
Whatever a childhood of old has to give?
You won't find it here, no laughter, no love

The wind drew closer, the leaves approached
I treaded carefully on dried spoken leaves
Fed with writings, they fell to the ground

"No laughter, no love is what you did gain
The evenings were fierce, the days were worse
But when does a flower that blooms not die?
And when does a storm that hits not cry?"

"Painful indeed were the days that went by
But healing is what you owe to yourself
Tempted to hold on, the anger, the red
But see how your sun can shine instead."

Abused without Cause

9

I did shine instead, my years that caught up
My work to show, a lot did I
I know the past is long far behind
The suns that shined burnt ages ago
The moons that lit up the nights have dimmed
down
And the rooms of a home that once were are no
more

So, how do I paint my life anew?
The short end of a straw was something I drew
This is how it has been, this is how I turned out
Their lessons, their concepts, the people, the
laws
What good can they do
When abused without cause?

For a Future Unseen

Yes, humans have long abused without cause
Like a waterfall, they flow without hesitation
As though it's okay to pour where they fall

I wonder why lives are okay with this living
That with goodbyes come an unending day

I wonder why lives are okay with the wrongs
That when one commits, the other is led astray

Reason did I try to make with them
That not all events are subtle and zen
With psychopaths holding the proverbial pen
They're writing my fate like it were their own

No control of their deeds or words
Just mindless decisions for a future unseen

The Words from their Ink

Yes, the future unseen is open to all
And yet my words were true
Forced out to the ends of a waterfall
A whirlwind had broken, the currents had
spoken

But knowing from where they came
The wind, this time, had something to say

"Don't let them tell you what you should do
Listen, take heed to all that is true
Good things will happen and a lot of bad
The reasons to which senses do not add
But still, tis your journey, your path to create"

"Whatever they've written cannot choose your
fate
It's only if you let them write on your pages
Believing their words, twisting the learnings of
the sages
That whatever had happened, the history in
those pages
Will make you do what they say, the words from
their ink"

Spring from Within

12

The words from their ink, different from mine
The diary of written letters to you
The diary given by you, and my words that
flowed

And when I wrote, the wind calmed down
The raging pain within me stopped
The heart that burned was cooler under water
The tears that flowed like rain on a sunny day

Much love has floated amid the clouds
Your wings have felt the warmth of the sun
I hope as you dwell up there
That my love for me will spring from within

Too Hard to Dwell

13

Whatever we'll have will spring from within
The heart will feel a subtle nudge
To rise above the pain and grudge

Isn't this what we always do?
Pointing fingers at me and you
But then your absence taught me well
That darkness inside is too hard to dwell

It can't stay inside, it has to come out
Where light that shatters is spread all about
Spiralling down can never be the same
As darkness inside is too hard to dwell

Waiting to Bloom

14

It is too hard to dwell on a loved one's loss
Or love that is lost
Standing on either side
Two worlds that cannot cross
No matter the cost

Life is such, it gives you the sun and the rain
It gives you the warmth and the pain
But even the day that meets its doom
There's a flower within waiting to bloom

Make the Sun Shine Today

15

"Why is it still waiting to bloom?"
Asked the wind in whispering leaves
"Your time has come, your time is now
There is no yesterday nor tomorrow
There is no joy, there is no pain
Just the living of today, and nothing less to gain"

I looked up at the sky
Tearing up above the clouds
Or were it my eyes that always welled up?

Then the wind said, "The way you see is what
you'll be
Why must you see the dark and grey?
When you can make the sun shine today"

Into Being

If I can make the sun shine today
Then so can I make the rains pour
Even if you are no more
My heart can beat still for you

The flowers bloomed when you smiled
Glowing now in your memories
I know life ripples across its forms

But life there, we all know it
It knows to take different shapes

Like the crouching tiger
It roars its breath into fiery storms
Like the leaves of Spring
Life can again come into being

Touched My Soul

17

And when fullness comes into being
We shall meet again
Until then my wings shall learn to take flight

I'll learn to cross the rivers of darkness
With the brightness of the sun
For your love has touched my soul

Let it Go

For when you touched my soul
I was born into your arms
My fears you kissed way at night
Even when you weren't in sight

My eyes could not see
But I know your smile was just for me
Our bond was strong even though apart
But love can find its way
Beneath the dark clouds or the crooked path

And even though my anger can be felt
Miles away from where I knelt
To the passing away of your life
The winds whispered away the pain
Telling me to let it go

Let it Melt

19

Let it go, the trauma, the void
The smouldering heat that destroyed
Let it go, I did, I tried

I realised that ships set sail
They float back, ships of wreck
From the past, they choke my neck
Rummaging through doors half open

But again, your smile has shown the way
That you are still there, around somewhere
Your life has simply passed from one world

We've met before, you and I
It's a matter of time before again
We meet when our lifetimes dock ashore

Lifetimes dock ashore

20

Let it melt, my tears of long ago
The fears of what may be
Let it melt like sugar on fire

For your smile was Caramel Love
It could wipe a million tears
And still glow through darker clouds

For your soul was the touch of an angel
That shone its light in the darkest of times
Your soul, the work of cherry blossoms

I wonder how we met
Or when did our souls connect
When did our lifetimes dock ashore?

Caramel Love

Indeed did our lifetimes dock ashore
When you prayed with eyes closed
Nestled in the shelter of your heart
Was the Mother Most Pure

When you prayed to the Seat of Wisdom
Birthed upon your blessings
You called upon me
Fed me in your loving arms

Thus, was I born, but you were my gift
Connected from one life to another
Our journeys coincided, our time was afloat

The journey may have ended
The darkness may have remained
The unseen clouds may have floated above
The treasure chest may have shut close

But it is never the start
Or end for souls eternal
For we will meet again
My sweet mother, my Caramel Love